Original title:
.Mischief and Magic: Tales of Elves

Copyright © 2024 Creative Arts Management OÜ
All rights reserved.

Author: Aidan Marlowe
ISBN HARDBACK: 978-9916-90-910-2
ISBN PAPERBACK: 978-9916-90-911-9

Whimsicals of the Elder Woods

In the woods where the squirrels wear shoes,
And the owls sing the latest news.
Mushrooms dance with hats so tall,
While rabbits play leapfrog at the fall.

The trees giggle, their leaves a-flutter,
As chipmunks gossip 'bout the nutty clutter.
Bunnies with glasses read ancient scrolls,
Joking about the world's silly roles.

Frogs in tuxedos serenade the moon,
With grace that makes the stars swoon.
Even the beetles march in line,
Chanting "Life is good, let's dine on brine!"

In this place of silly charms,
Where nature's quirks catch us off-guard alarms.
Join the fun, take off your shoes,
In Elder Woods, here's always good news!

The Craft of Calamity Among the Fae

In a land where fairies wear mismatched socks,
They brew tea in kooky, oversized rocks.
With wands made of candy and dreams so grand,
They paint rainbows with a flick of hand.

But oh! A mishap in the faerie's brew,
Turned cupcakes into frogs and frogs into stew!
Now cupcakes hop and frogs sing high,
Causing the woodland critters to sigh.

The gnomes chuckle as chaos unfolds,
Trading tales of calamity so bold.
One fairy tried to bake a pie,
But ended up with a dragonfly!

Yet their laughter rings beneath the trees,
As they dodge pesky bees and a teasing breeze.
In faerie lands of whimsy and cheer,
A little folly is worth the cheer!

Trickster's Serenade Among the Trees

In the woods where squirrels scheme,
A raccoon plots a heist supreme.
He swipes the snacks from picnics near,
And laughs beneath the moonlit sphere.

A deer with antlers topped in gold,
Reveals a prank that's yet untold.
He jumps, he prances, and then he spins,
Says, 'Catch me if you can, my friends!'

The owls hoot spells of merry glee,
As shadows dance among the trees.
With every rustle, giggles grow,
A laughing wind begins to blow.

So wander forth, join in the fun,
For trickster tales have just begun.
With nature's charm and playful tease,
Life's a jester's song among the trees.

A Brew of Laughter and Light

In a cauldron bubbling bright,
Frogs are singing, what a sight!
They whirled and twirled in cheer and glee,
To brew up laughs with honey tea.

A witch concocts a joyous blend,
With giggles that just never end.
She stirs in jokes, a sprinkle of pun,
And serves it fresh to everyone.

Fairies dance on mushroom tops,
While elves in mischief never stop.
They sip the potion, twinkling eyes,
Exchanging giggles, blissful sighs.

At twilight's fall, the laughter swells,
As woodland folk weave funny spells.
With every sip of frothy delight,
They toast to joy beneath the night.

The Cunning Charm of Woodland Spirits

Among the trees, with shadows deep,
Woodland spirits laugh and leap.
With twinkles bright, they weave their charm,
Ensuring nature stays warm.

A gnome pops out from under bark,
With jokes that land like a funny spark.
He claims his beard is made of gold,
But knows it's only stories told.

The pixies prance on pulses swift,
Each giggle's a most precious gift.
They sprinkle dust of cheer and light,
To keep our smiles shining bright.

So heed the whispers of the woods,
Where laughter grows in hidden hoods.
With every rustle, charm takes flight,
And joy reigns true through day and night.

Secrets of the Glimmering Hollow

In the hollow, shiny and bright,
Hidden secrets spark delight.
Glimmers dance on emerald leaves,
While chuckles swirl like summer breeze.

A turtle tells a silly tale,
Of swimming faster than a snail.
The rabbits roll and chortle too,
For every jest they know is true.

A fox with mischief on his mind,
Plays pranks that leave the others blind.
He winks and slyly disappears,
Then reappears with goofy cheers.

So venture forth to where they play,
In the glimmering hollow, bright as day.
With laughter echoing through the trees,
Where secrets dance on the playful breeze.

The Prankster's Festival Under the Stars

Under the moonlight, mischief brews,
Jellybean rain and sticky blue goo.
From trees they swing, with a giggle and cheer,
Silly string flings; oh dear, oh dear!

A clown on a wagon, a chicken on skis,
Dancing around like he's lost in the breeze.
With pies in the face, and a bucket of weep,
The night whispers laughter; it's hard not to leap!

Who moved my cheese? The sly raccoon grins,
While the pig on a unicycle spins!
The prankster's delight, they gather 'round,
With gales of laughter, in joy they are drowned.

So bring on the chaos, let the games commence,
For under the stars, there's no need for pretense.
Just laughter and joy, till the dawn breaks anew,
At the prankster's festival, where fun's on the menu!

Luminous Larks of the Woodland Way

In a forest so bright, the larks take flight,
With glow-in-the-dark wings, a hilarious sight.
Singing to critters with giggles and glee,
A party of lights, as absurd as can be!

They dance on the branches, a comical show,
Flapping and flailing, they're putting on a flow.
Twinkling like stars, they float and they fly,
While squirrels compete in a race to the sky.

A hedgehog in glasses is cheering them on,
With jellybeans scattered, his trail's nearly gone.
They sing and they swirl, like bubbles in drinks,
Making merry up high, where the funny bird winks.

So come join the jest in the shimmering wood,
With larks and their antics, life's perfectly good.
Under the treetops, their laughter will sway,
In the playful embrace of the woodland way!

Fables Spun in Gossamer Threads

Once in a village, where tales weave and twine,
Lived a cat with a hat, yes, a hat that would shine.
He told tall tales of mice that would dance,
While squirrels in pajamas took daring romance!

A dog in a bowtie would fiddle and play,
As beavers debated their plans for the day.
With gossamer threads, these fables unfold,
Of dragons that sneeze and of knights who are bold.

The cow that jumped high went on quite a spree,
With chickens that clucked math — oh how they'd agree!

Each story a giggle, a chuckle, a grin,
Where whimsy and wonder were always within.

So listen, dear friend, to the yarns that we spin,
Of a world full of laughter, where joy does begin.
In fables spun lightly, your dreams will take flight,
With gossamer threads that shine brilliantly bright!

The Echoes of an Elven Laughter

In the glens of the forest, where secrets align,
Elves giggle and whisper, 'Is this grape or is it wine?'
They dance with the daisies, sing soft little tunes,
While fairies toast marshmallows with glowing gloons!

With their pointed hats, and a wink of the eye,
They'll play pranks on the trolls and share laughter so spry.
From the cradle of oaks, the echoes resound,
As joy spills like nectar all over the ground!

A riddle or two, just to keep you on toes,
Why did the mushroom go to the party? Who knows!
But laughter is magic, it twinkles like stars,
While elves paint the skies with their squeaks and guitars.

So if you should wander through woodlands so bright,
And hear laughter ring out through the soft veil of night,
Know the elves are just playing, their joy full and clear,
In echoes of laughter that all can endear!

Lanterns of Laughter and Shadows

In a town where giggles thrive,
Lanterns glowed, the jokes arrived.
Monsters danced in silly socks,
While shadows played with laughing clocks.

A cat wore glasses, quite absurd,
Claimed he could read every word.
The moon chuckled, a silver gleam,
At all the silliness, it seemed.

Puddles splashed with joyful splatters,
As everyone laughed at silly platters.
Even the broom joined in the fun,
Swaying left and right, with everyone.

So if you find a lantern bright,
Know laughter's hiding in plain sight.
Join the dance, don't be shy,
In this town, we all just fly!

The Mischievous Bloom

In a garden, blooms took flight,
Tickling noses, what a sight!
Daisies whispered silly rhymes,
While tulips danced in silly chimes.

A sunflower wore a polka dot,
Claimed it was the silliest spot.
Roses rolled and laughed in hue,
Spreading joy with every dew.

Petals pranked the bumblebees,
Hiding honey with such ease.
"Oh dear!" buzzed the flustered crew,
"Where's our snack? We're quite askew!"

So if you stroll by this mad patch,
With giggles trailing every catch,
Join the blooms, lose all that gloom,
And laugh along with the mischievous bloom!

Jests of the Woodland Spirits

In the woods where whispers tease,
Spirits giggle among the trees.
They throw acorns and prank the deer,
Making sure laughter's always near.

A squirrel dons a tiny hat,
Chasing shadows, imagine that!
While fairies ride on toadstool trains,
Singing songs of silly pains.

The owls hoot in cheeky tones,
Joining in with silly moans.
A chipmunk juggles berries bright,
Under the watch of the moonlight.

So tiptoe softly, don't disturb,
These woodland jesters, how they curb.
Join their fun, don't stand and pout,
In the woods, laughter's the route!

Rebellion in the Fairy Ring

In a circle of mushrooms so round,
Fairies plot with leaps and bounds.
No more rules and no more ties,
It's time for pranks and funny lies!

One fairy swapped her wand for cake,
Proclaiming laughter's all it takes.
While others turned their hats to flowers,
Transforming giggles into powers.

They painted rocks in polka dots,
And shuffled about in silly knots.
"Oh no!" cried one with wobbly wings,
"Life's too short for boring things!"

So if you find this fairy site,
Where rebellion glows with pure delight,
Join the ring, no need to cling,
To giggles born from the fairy zing!

Revelry in the Midnight Glade

In the midnight glade, the squirrels dance,
With acorn hats, they take their chance.
Bunnies join in with a flair for the fun,
While wise old owls just watch, on the run.

Mice play fiddles made of twigs and yarn,
The moonlight bathes them, a gentle charm.
Every shadow wiggles, every branch sways,
Under the glow, they forget their days.

A raccoon in shades leads the silly band,
Tapping on trees with a wooden hand.
As laughter echoes through the leafy maze,
Even grumpy bears can't help but gaze.

So grab your snacks, come join the spree,
In the glade of wonder, so wild and free.
With nature's laughter under starlit skies,
The fun never ends—just look at their eyes!

Echoes of the Forest Frolic.

In the forest deep, where the wild things play,
Frogs in tuxedos leap and sway.
Toads join the mix with a croaky croon,
They host a gala beneath the moon.

Squirrels debate 'bout the best nut cuisine,
While chipmunks argue if it's all a dream.
Hedgehogs spin tales of their daring trips,
Each story gets louder with exaggerated flips.

A dance-off unfolds on the soft mossy floor,
Chickadees chirp as they ask for encore.
Raccoons in sequins throw glittery throws,
While deer just ponder what everybody knows.

Laughter resounds through the thick ancient trees,
Echoes of joy carried on the breeze.
With nature as witness to the grand jubilee,
The forest's alive, come join in, whee!

Whispers in the Moonlit Grove

In the moonlit grove, secrets are shared,
Where foxes and badgers have never cared.
With tails all a-twirl, they plot and scheme,
While fireflies wink like a mischievous dream.

Owls hoot advice on the best midnight snack,
Chipmunks pack sandwiches, ready to crack.
Every whisper echoes through the tall trees,
Like bedtime stories, but with slight unease.

A raccoon chef cooks with flair and style,
His famous bug stew makes everyone smile.
As shadows shimmy to the rhythm of night,
Even the crickets join in the delight.

So slip on your shoes, let's dance under stars,
With woodland buddies, no need for cars.
In this magical grove where the laughter roves,
Every giggle assures us of stories in droves.

Enchanted Secrets of the Sylvan Realm

In the sylvan realm, where mischief runs free,
Elves play hide-and-seek, with glee by the tree.
Pixies zoom past like a spark in the dark,
While gnomes trade tales of their hometown park.

A squirrel writes poems with acorn ink,
Spinning wild tales that make you think.
Fairies quack up with a jolly good laugh,
At every tall tale that draws a big gasp.

Mushrooms parade in their colorful dress,
Each one a dancer, creating a mess.
The glowworms twinkle, keeping the beat,
As frogs in top hats make life truly sweet.

So bring your snacks and your brightest smile,
Join in the fun, stay for a while.
In this enchanted place, where the magic flows,
Every moment here is anything goes!

The Forest's Mischievous Heart

In the forest, shadows dance,
Squirrels plotting in a trance.
They steal pebbles, oh so sly,
While owl hoots a watchful eye.

Bunnies bounce on hidden trails,
Whiskers twitching, leave no trails.
Frogs wear hats, parade in line,
While fireflies sip on moonshine.

Raccoons tumble, what a sight,
Juggling acorns, pure delight.
A leaf slips, and down they go,
Laughter echoes, all aglow.

Under stars, they cozy up,
Sharing tales and teasing pup.
Nature giggles, joins the fun,
The day ends, but mischief's spun.

Enchanted Lullabies from Starlit Halls

In a treehouse 'neath the moon,
Crickets play a sleepy tune.
Frogs croon soft with sleepy eyes,
As the stars begin to rise.

Moonbeams glide on silken streams,
Singing lullabies of dreams.
Owls recite the tales of night,
While fireflies twinkle, soft and bright.

Squirrels nest with blankets warm,
Building forts, a cozy swarm.
Tree branches sway, whispering low,
To the sleepy world below.

Starlit halls of nature's glee,
Cradle life in harmony.
Close your eyes, let laughter flow,
Through the magic, let dreams grow.

The Jinks of Jolly Sylphs

In the glade, where laughter rings,
Sylphs are prancing, flapping wings.
They tickle toadstools, play a game,
Whisper secrets, never tame.

With a giggle, they take flight,
Painting clouds with pure delight.
Chasing shadows, wild and free,
Dancing 'round the old oak tree.

One trips over a bumpy root,
Landing right in a squirrel's hoot.
Their laughter bubbles, spreads like bread,
As they mimic the snoozing dead.

Night descends, and mischief swells,
In the air, a tale it tells.
For in the woods, where joy entwines,
Jolly sylphs weave the best designs.

Tales from the Sylvan Mischief Makers

Whispers float on a twilight breeze,
Foxes gossiping 'neath tall trees.
With a wink and a knowing grin,
They plot mischief, let the fun begin.

Rabbits race with painted tails,
As fairies tell their funny tales.
Gnomes wear shoes two sizes too wide,
Tripping over pride in the woodsy slide.

Butterflies wear hats on their wings,
While grasshoppers chirp and sing.
Crickets crack jokes, they can't be beat,
As raccoons dance on tiny feet.

As night falls, echoes resound,
A symphony of giggles all around.
In this realm of leafy cheer,
Mischief's heart keeps drawing near.

Luminous Trickery in Hoarfrost Woods

In hoarfrost woods where shadows play,
A squirrel in goggles shouts hooray!
He skates on ice with merry glee,
While pine trees dance, so wild and free.

A fox in shoes, quite out of place,
Chases his tail at a breakneck pace!
The owl rolls eyes, a sarcastic hoot,
As rabbit sports an oversized boot.

Beneath the glow of chilly moons,
They sing to Sunday afternoon tunes.
With every jab and playful jest,
These woodland critters know the best.

So if you venture, take a peek,
Where laughter lives and mischief's meek.
Just beware the tricks that sneak on by,
In hoarfrost woods, where giggles fly!

A Sylvan Story of Whimsy and Glee

In a woodland glade with joy galore,
A deer wears glasses, what a bore!
She reads a book about the stars,
While chipmunks toast with acorn jars.

A party held beneath a tree,
Where raccoons dance with wild decree.
They toss confetti, made of leaves,
And celebrate what joy believes.

A hedgehog spins, a ballerina's dream,
While fireflies twinkle, a bright team.
The trees all sway, they can't resist,
This sylvan tale of whimsy kissed.

So if you hear a giggle or two,
Just stop and look at what they do!
These merry friends, both small and tall,
Create a world where dreams enthrall.

Tales of Trickery and Starlight

In moonlit glens where stories brew,
A cat tells tales of what he knew.
He claims he caught a shooting star,
  But it just giggled and flew far.

A rabbit dressed like a magician,
Pulls carrots from a top hat—vision!
The audience of frogs all croak,
  They can't decide if it's a joke.

The owls play poker, silent as night,
While fireflies twinkle, oh, what a sight!
With every trick and playful tease,
  The woods erupt in fits of wheeze.

So gather 'round, let tales spin bright,
Of trickery and whimsical light.
For in this glade, with every yawn,
  The laughter echoes till the dawn!

The Glint of Laughter Beneath Leaf and Stone

Beneath the leaves, where shadows creep,
A funky worm begins to leap.
With tiny shades and disco flair,
He throws a party, unaware of care.

The hedgehogs join, with bopping heads,
As squirrels twirl on mossy beds.
All nature sings a silly tune,
At midnight's dance beneath the moon.

A frog jumps high; it's quite the sight,
He lands on a stag, just right—oh, right!
And laughter echoes through the glen,
As friends unite, time and again.

So if you wander to this scene,
With giggles bright and moments keen,
Remember there's more than meets the eye,
In playful woods where spirits fly!

Whirlwind Tales from Mischievous Spirits

In a forest deep, the spirits dance,
Twirling about in a silly prance.
They trip on roots and laugh with glee,
A raucous show, so wild and free.

One spritely sprite caught a frog by mistake,
He tickled its tummy, for a little break.
The frog leapt high with a ribbiting cheer,
The spirit just squealed, 'Come back here, dear!'

They chased around till the sun was bright,
Bumping and bouncing, what a sight!
With a hop and a skip, they vanish at dusk,
Leaving behind a sweet scent of musk.

So next time you wander where shadows fall,
Look out for the spirits—don't trip, that's all!
They'll wink and they'll giggle, and if you get wise,
You might just join in on their silly disguise.

Mirth and Merriment in Nature's Heart

A squirrel in a hat, oh what a sight,
Hosting a party under the moonlight.
With acorns for snacks and berries for wine,
The critters all laughed, feeling divine.

A rabbit tap dances, paws up in the air,
While the raccoons hustle, with style and flair.
The owls provide music, hooting a beat,
As nature celebrates, it's quite the feat!

They juggle some nuts, creating a mess,
But giggles explode; they don't care, no stress.
With friends all around, the joy is contagious,
In this wild woodland, it's simply outrageous!

So if you find laughter beneath the oak tree,
Join in the fun, wild and carefree.
For in nature's heart where mirth takes the lead,
Every day's a party—oh, yes indeed!

A Tangle of Tricky Elfin Tales

In the land of the elves, tricks are a game,
Where jests and jives are the source of their fame.
They hide all the spoons, and the forks on a whim,
Leaving the humans confused and grim.

A tiny elf giggled, his face full of cheer,
As he turned all the cows into fluffy deer.
The farmers awoke with a blink of their eyes,
To find their cows bouncing—oh what a surprise!

They turned the rivers to chocolate delight,
Making even the fish swim with pure fright.
Waving their wands with nimble finesse,
They laughed at the chaos, causing distress.

Yet when the sun sets and night draws near,
The elves gather 'round with hearts full of cheer.
They share all their tales, both funny and bright,
In a tangle of laughter, pure love, and light.

Songs of Sprightly Echoes and Whimsy

In a meadow where laughter hangs sweet like the air,
Sprightly echoes of whimsy float everywhere.
A butterfly wearing a bright little tie,
Sings tunes that make daisies begin to sigh.

The bumblebees hum with a jazzy beat,
While crickets chirp softly, their song so sweet.
A hedgehog in shades does the cha-cha with glee,
As the sun sets low, it's a wild jubilee!

Mice in the grass host a fancy soirée,
Inviting all critters for a dance and a play.
With cheese on the table and jokes on each plate,
The laughter rolls on—oh, it's never too late!

So listen for echoes of laughter and cheer,
In the songs that are sung, from creatures so dear.
For whimsy is woven in life's tapestry,
A sprightly reminder of joy, wild and free!

Secrets of the Mischievous Treetop

In the treetops high, where the squirrels play,
They throw acorns down, in a cheeky way.
The birds roll their eyes, as they dodge the rain,
While fairies chuckle, in delightful disdain.

One raccoon climbs up, with a hat made of leaves,
He twirls and he spins, oh, how he deceives.
With a wink and a nod, he steals snacks from a picnic,
Causing all the folks to feel quite a bit thick.

A wise old owl gives a hoot of surprise,
As the mischief unfolds right before his wise eyes.
But he's not too bothered, he's seen all this play,
In the secrets of treetops, mischief's the way!

So next time you wander beneath the green dome,
Remember those critters who call treetops home.
They're plotting and laughing, in their leafy retreat,
Sharing the secrets that make life so sweet!

A Jester's Journey Through Faerie Realms

A jester with bells, and a grin ear to ear,
Took a trip to the fae, with his heart full of cheer.
He juggled some mushrooms, and danced near a brook,
While fairies all giggled, too shy for a look.

He met a pink dragon, who sneezed out some spark,
And in clouds of glitter, they danced till it's dark.
They played hide and seek, 'neath a rainbow's bright arc,
But the faeries kept winning, they were here with a spark!

With a splat and a plop, he fell into mud,
"Oh dear!" said the jester, as he looked like a dud.
The faeries just laughed, with a twinkle in sight,
As they sent him on home, in a whirl of delight.

But as he departed, with a wink and a pun,
He vowed to return, oh, this was too fun!
For in faerie realms, where mischief takes a stand,
The jester found joy, and a scattered magic band.

Revelry in the Realm of Enchantment

In the realm of enchantment, where giggles take flight,
There's a party of pixies that lasts through the night.
With cakes made of starlight and juice from the moon,
They dance on the breezes, from dusk until noon.

A gnome plays the tuba, while trolls tap their feet,
As the fairies do cartwheels, what a whimsical feat!
They twirl and they whirl, in a dazzling display,
Not a single soul's grumpy, they're all here to play.

But watch out for sprites, they're the tricky little fools,
They might swap your dessert for a bowl made of jewels.
With a wink and a giggle, they vanish from sight,
Leaving laughter behind, in the soft starlit night.

So join in the revelry, embrace all the cheer,
In the realm of enchantment, there's magic right here.
With friends all around, and mischief galore,
In this lively domain, you'll be wishing for more!

The Harmony of Elusive Echoes

In the woods where echoes play, a tale takes its flight,
A chorus of giggles sings through day and night.
With each rustle of leaves, secrets whisper with glee,
As the shadows sway gently, like notes on a spree.

The rabbits tap dance on the tips of their toes,
While a wise tortoise teaches them how to pose.
A melody of mischief in every soft breeze,
As the flora and fauna unite with the trees.

Yet lurking nearby, a grouchy old fox,
Dreams of quiet, while the others are in frocks.
But the harmony swells, as friends pull him in,
With a grin he admits, "Well, I'll join in the din!"

So listen dear friend, to the echoes that call,
There's laughter and joy in the heart of them all.
The harmony lingers, elusive and bright,
In the woods where the echoes paint day into night.

Chronicles of the Winking Woods

In the woods where the trees do wink,
Squirrels plot with a knowing blink.
They steal from the birdfeeders high,
While birds squawk, 'Hey, that's not so fly!'

Acorns roll like marbles at play,
Rabbits bounce in a clumsy ballet.
The wise old owl pretends to snooze,
While chipmunks plan their acorn cruise.

Glimmers of mischief fill the air,
As raccoons raid without a care.
Beneath the moon, they dance and prance,
In the winking woods, all take a chance!

When dawn breaks, it's quite a sight,
Squirrels in pajamas, what a delight!
If you stop to see this curious spree,
You might just join their wild jubilee!

Flickering Secrets of the Autumn Leaves

Leaves whisper secrets as they fall,
Dancing around, they answer the call.
Golden hues twirl in the breeze,
While crickets strum tunes with ease.

A squirrel dons a leaf as a hat,
While birds gossip, 'What do you think of that?'
Pumpkins giggle under their vines,
Wondering if they'll soon drink wines.

The wind takes a funny little twist,
As branches shake and twigs persist.
They tickle the noses of those who stroll,
Leaving them laughing, feeling whole.

So stroll through autumn, let laughter lead,
With each crunch beneath, feel joy proceed.
For in the flickering light, we see,
A world where leaves share their comedy!

The Enchanted Trickster's Dance

In the moonlight, shadows prance,
A trickster whispers, 'Join the dance!'
Fairies giggle, filling the air,
While goblins trip over their own hair.

The stars above start to sway,
As creatures plot their own cabaret.
Mice in suits, wearing real ties,
Twirl and spin 'neath the laughing skies.

With pies that sing and cakes that prance,
The enchanted night gives all a chance.
Dancing wild with glittered glee,
In the forest, all are carefree.

But beware the prank of a wise old fox,
He'll steal your shoes or hide your socks!
Yet laughter binds us, friends all around,
In this enchanted dance, joy is found!

The Pantomime of Petal-Whispers

Petals flutter with a soft, sweet sigh,
In gardens where the giggling bees fly.
A rose whispers secrets, soft and grand,
As flowers in bloom all join the band.

Tulips gossip of their favorite song,
While daisies dance, all merry and strong.
The violets wink, pushing petals wide,
In a colorful show, they take great pride.

Butterflies flit, adding to the flair,
With a pirouette in the sunlit air.
The daisies cheer, 'Don't let this stop!'
As butterflies land, never a flop.

As twilight falls, the flowers still play,
In their pantomime, they sway and sway.
For in this garden, where laughter swirls,
Petal-whispers weave joy for all girls and boys!

The Wisp's Playful Gauntlet

In the meadow where shadows prance,
The wisps frolic, a whimsical dance.
They twirl and tease, like playful sprites,
Guiding the lost on clever flights.

With lanterns made of giggles bright,
They spark the dark with sheer delight.
"Follow us, silly!" they gleefully cry,
But trip on a root, oh me, oh my!

They'll lead you to a banquet fair,
With jellybeans that float in air.
But don't eat too much, take heed, my friend,
For the wisp's wild games might never end!

Now you've danced through the playful night,
Best to leave before dawn's first light.
With laughter trailing, you'll run back home,
But don't forget your froggy foam!

Adventures in Dreamweaver's Forest

In Dreamweaver's Forest, dreams take flight,
With dancing trees and stars so bright.
You'll meet a rabbit in a bow tie,
Who winks and whispers, "Give it a try!"

The flowers giggle with hues so loud,
Trying to out-laugh the butterfly crowd.
They tickle your feet as you walk on through,
While clouds throw pies, a sweet, sticky brew!

Beware the squirrels, with acorn hats,
They plot with charm, like sneaky cats.
Their treasure maps lead to chaotic fun,
An endless chase, never to shun.

As night descends, the shadows grow,
With mischievous sprites putting on a show.
A dreamer's laugh, a wisp of glee,
In this forest of wonders, you'll always be free!

The Jester's Gift of Enchantment

A jester came with bells that jingle,
His trickster grin made all hearts tingle.
He twirled a hat that floated high,
And pulled a rabbit that seemed to fly!

With painted cheeks and antics galore,
He juggled pies and begged for more.
"Catch these treats if you dare!" he cried,
As whipped cream splattered, oh what a ride!

A card trick here, a riddle there,
He spun the crowd in fits of laughter and flair.
But when his pants fell with an alarming sound,
The uproarious joy was utterly profound!

So if you see him on the way,
Join his circus, don't delay.
For laughter's a gift, oh what a thrill,
In the jester's world, you'll always fill!

Sylvan Whimsies in the Night

In the woods where critters put on a show,
The owls proclaim, "Come join the flow!"
A raccoon with shades plays a sweet guitar,
While fireflies flicker like tiny stars.

The mushrooms gather for a weird ballet,
With toads on the sidelines shouting, "Hooray!"
They leap with splendor, somewhat askew,
While dancing with shadows in a shimmery hue.

An owl spins tales of ancient lore,
While nightingales serenade, always wanting more.
They swoop and dive, a melodic flight,
In sylvan whimsies beneath the night.

So bring your laughter, your heart, your cheer,
Join this spectacle that brings you near.
For in these woods, dreams take their flight,
In whimsical wonders that ignite the night!

Shadows of Play in the Moonlit Wood

In the woods where shadows creep,
Silly squirrels play hide and seek.
One rolled over with a squeak,
The owls just giggled, 'What a freak!'

A rabbit wearing a tiny hat,
Tripped on a branch, how about that?
The moonlight shone on his little spat,
And all the critters laughed, 'Imagine that!'

Frogs serenade with croaks so grand,
While raccoons set up a rock band.
In this forest, life's unplanned,
The mischief twirls like grains of sand.

As night winds down, they can't delay,
The shadows promise they'll come out to play.
With laughter echoing 'til it's day,
In moonlit woods, where dreams ballet.

The Curious Chronicles of Forest Sprites

Once a sprite with shoes of gold,
Thought he was brave and oh so bold.
But tripped on roots that life had scrolled,
Now tales of clumsiness are retold.

With giggles, pixies threw a feast,
Dancing round the silly beast.
The ants arrived, their snacks increased,
Serving crumbs, they were quite pleased.

One sprite tried to catch a butterfly,
But fell face-first; oh my, oh my!
The flower laughed, 'You missed, oh why?'
The forest's cheer made spirits fly.

Their friendship sparkles like sunlit dew,
In these woods, oddities brew.
With every laugh, they start anew,
In curious tales of the merry crew!

The Dance of the Wayward Wisp

A wisp wandered late, feeling spry,
Led by the glow of a firefly.
'Oh dear, am I really supposed to fly?'
It danced through branches with a sigh.

The moon chuckled, 'What a sight!'
As wisp spun 'round in pure delight.
It twirled and twirled, then took a bite,
Of a shadow that was not so bright.

Bumblebees joined in the fun,
Decked in pollen, they laughed and run.
The forest echoed, 'A dance we shun!'
'But, oh dear wisp, you've really won!'

Now every night, they gather again,
To dance under stars, their joy a pen.
For in the wild, laughter's the zen,
With a wayward wisp, and friends 'til then.

Echoes of Playfulness in the Glen

In a glen where echoes bounce,
Bunnies hop and squirrels pounce.
With every leap, they sing and flounce,
While frogs croak tunes; what a pronounc!

A hedgehog strolled with style and grace,
Kicking up leaves in a wild race.
His friends all laughed and changed their pace,
Joining the march, making a base.

The wind blew softly, a playful tease,
Whispering secrets to all with ease.
In the glen, where joy's a breeze,
They rolled and tumbled, hearts pleased.

As daylight wanes, the echoes yell,
'Time for more fun, there's no farewell!'
With giggles ringing like a sweet bell,
In this glen, they know play very well.

Spirited Flights through Whispering Pines

A squirrel wore goggles, flying very high,
With nuts for fuel, it touched the sky.
The birds were jealous, squawking in dismay,
While trees waved branches, cheering all the way.

A raccoon in a cape, zoomed past with flair,
Exclaiming, "I'm the hero!" while stealing a pear.
Pines danced with laughter, as the day took flight,
In a wild game of tag that lasted till night.

A chipmunk chef served acorn pâté,
Critters gathered 'round for the feast of the day.
They clinked tiny cups, made of pinecone,
Giggles echoing through the woods, all alone.

As the sun dipped low, shadows began to play,
A racquetball match, with shadows on display.
With giggles and squeals, the forest came alive,
In spirited flights, nature takes a dive!

Shadows of Frolic in Faerie Land

In Faerie Land, where the shadows prance,
Pixies put on a tango dance.
With twirls and sparkles, they swept through air,
Even the daisies got caught in their flair.

A gnome in a hat, ten sizes too big,
Tried to impress with a tap-dance jig.
But tripped on his boots, into thorns he fell,
A soft-spoken hedgehog laughed, "All's well!"

The mushrooms chuckled, their caps bobbing high,
As fairies whispered secrets, giggling nearby.
"I saw a troll trying to bake a pie!"
"Is it true?" "Oh yes!" "Let's go see! Oh my!"

With light on their wings, they flitted away,
To check on the troll at the end of the day.
In shadows of frolic, beneath the moonlight,
Life is a dance, a whimsical flight!

The Glimmering Path of the Trickster

On the glimmering path, where antics abound,
A fox in a bowtie pranced all around.
His tail held high, he played hide-and-seek,
With rabbits who giggled from behind a creek.

A raccoon with shades was the judge of the fun,
While squirrels debated who was fastest to run.
"Not I!" said the turtle, then blinked with a grin,
"Let's race to the finish, and just let me win!"

A chortle broke loose from a nearby tree,
As a parrot squawked, "Join the jamboree!"
With pies flying high, and laughter in strides,
The glimmering path basked in joy's wild tides.

Every mischief, every prank,
Added to friendships, and laughter tanked.
So follow the path where the tricksters play,
In corners of joy, that brighten the day!

Whimsy and Wonder Beneath the Oaks

Beneath ancient oaks, where the wild things roam,
A bear wore a scarf, claiming it's home.
With honey sandwiches, he offered a bite,
While raccoons debated what's wrong and what's right.

A turtle in spectacles, reading a book,
Says, "The secret to life is in every nook!"
The owls hooted softly, ''We're wise; don't you see?"
While squirrels clutched popcorn, watching for free.

A moose dressed in bowties strutted with pride,
Critters all cheered, "Let's take a ride!"
An impromptu parade, with giggles and glee,
Whimsy and wonder danced free as can be.

So gather your pals, and join the parade,
Under the oaks, where the magic is made.
With tales to share, and laughs all around,
Beneath ancient oaks, pure joy can be found!

The Elixir of Delight in Eldern Woods

In Eldern Woods where fairies roam,
They brew a drink that tastes like foam.
With giggles bright and voices loud,
They serve it up to all the crowd.

A sip of joy, a splash of glee,
It makes the trees dance, can't you see?
The squirrels join in, a raucous cheer,
While rabbits laugh till they shed a tear.

With every glance, a wink they share,
It tickles hearts; there's magic there.
For in these woods, delight's a goal,
An elixir that can soothe the soul.

So if you seek a quirk or two,
Just wander where the wildflowers grew.
Taste the laughter, let it ignite,
The elixir of delight feels so right!

The Playful Mirth of the Fey

In a glen where fey folk play,
They joke and caper through the day.
With fairy dust and winked-out eyes,
They spin tall tales and silly lies.

A mushroom hat, a toadstool dance,
Each moment sparkles, a dreamlike chance.
They play pranks on the passing deer,
Whispers of laughter only they hear.

From dawn till dusk, they frolic and tease,
Climbing high in branches, just to appease.
They chase the sun, they hide the moon,
In their merry world, there's always room.

So if you wander through the vale,
Do join the fey, you cannot fail.
With playful mirth, they'll share their fun,
The laughter echoes, never done!

Twinkling Mischief in the Fairy Ring

In a circle bright, the fairies dance,
With twinkling eyes and a playful glance.
They stir the air with giggling sound,
Creating mischief all around.

They tie the shoes of passing folk,
And chuckle loud at every joke.
A flutter here, a whisper there,
Their giggles filling fragrant air.

Hiding behind a mossy stone,
They plot and scheme while feeling grown.
With every twirl and dizzy spin,
The mischief bubbles up within.

So step inside their magic ring,
Embrace the joys their frolics bring.
In twinkling mischief, laughter sings,
A fairy world with endless springs!

Legends of Laughter in the Leafy Glade

In the leafy glade, a tale unwinds,
Of legendary laughs and playful minds.
The trees all chuckle, branches sway,
As critters gather for another day.

With acorn hats and twiggy shoes,
They sing of fun and joyful news.
The breezes carry their crazy sounds,
As hilarity in nature abounds.

Through every giggle, adventure grows,
While silly stories twist and flow.
The paths they roam are lined with cheer,
With nightfall bringing that fey frontier.

So come and join this merry parade,
In the leafy glade where glee's displayed.
Legends of laughter fill the air,
A timeless echo of joy to share!

Whispers in the Moonlit Grove

In the moonlight, owls take flight,
They hoot and swoop with delight.
Squirrels debate, "Is that a cat?"
While frogs wear hats and dance like that!

Beneath the stars, the shadows play,
Rabbits gossip, "Where's the hay?"
A raccoon juggles shiny spoons,
As crickets serenade the tunes.

Trees giggle as the breeze rolls by,
Whispering secrets to the sky.
"Did you hear that? A laugh or two!"
"Let's peek, my friend, what's he up to?"

So in the grove, where laughs are found,
The animals gather, joy unbound.
Moonlit mischief fills the night,
With whispers of pure delight!

The Trickster's Lullaby

Socks disappear, oh what a sight!
The cat's on a mission, all through the night.
Elves are dancing 'round the bed,
With tiny giggles filling your head.

While you dream of candy, bright and sweet,
A squirrel's plotting a nut-filled treat.
He switches your sweets for acorns instead,
Laughing and shaking his tiny head.

Teddy bears gather for a chat,
Complaining about the sleeping brat.
With pillows as shields, they plot and scheme,
In the world of dreams, nothing's as it seems.

So dream away in the moonlit glow,
But beware of the tricksters, they're in the know!
With a wink, they vanish, leaving just a sigh,
Fall asleep, dear child, to the trickster's lullaby.

Secrets of the Enchanted Glade

In the glade where flowers bloom,
Pixies giggle, dispelling gloom.
Butterflies wear capes of gold,
While gnomes tell tales never old.

"Who left the cake out? I did hear!"
Squeaky mice, with wide-eyed cheer.
They nibble crumbs and leap about,
Whispering secrets, oh what a rout!

Toads in bow ties slide on the grass,
While the frogs take bets on who'll fall last.
A weasel brings snacks, oh so divine,
As fairies toast with elderflower wine.

But of all the secrets, one stands tall,
A magic spell with a bounce and a call.
Gather 'round, for it's time to play,
In the heart of the glade on this splendid day!

Pranks of the Starry Fae

Beneath the stars, the fae convene,
With glittery tricks, they're quite the scene.
A light bulb goes pop! A total surprise,
As fireflies dance with giggling sighs.

They swap the moon with a disco ball,
Lighting up mushrooms, dancing tall.
Gremlins slide down, all in a flurry,
With glitter bombs causing sweet worry.

At midnight, the stars hold their breath,
As faeries create mischief, feeling blessed.
They swap the sun with a bright red shoe,
And chuckle loud, as they bid adieu.

So beware when shadows play at night,
The starry fae are filled with delight.
For laughter blooms where dreams abound,
In the pranks of the fae, joy can be found!

Where the Fireflies Dance and Play

In twilight's glow, they flicker bright,
With tiny hats, oh what a sight!
They twirl and swirl in buzzing glee,
A dance-off held by yonder tree.

They giggle softly, oh such fun,
As they play tag, one by one.
A clumsy bug trips, falls in the mud,
Now he's a glowworm, not a stud!

When morning comes, the fun must cease,
But don't you worry, it's no big tease.
They'll be back soon, just wait and see,
To throw a bash, just them and me!

So when you spot their tiny lights,
Join the party, share the sights.
For where fireflies dance, joy's on the way,
Come join the laugh while they sway and play!

The Prank of the Woodland Warden

Old Warden Woodrow wore a sly grin,
He'd plant a whoopee cushion, let the laughs begin!
Rabbits hop, and the owls hoot,
As squirrels fall from trees in dispute.

He tickles the fawns with a feathered quill,
While the hedgehogs attempt to stand still.
But when they trip and roll in a heap,
Woodrow chuckles, then takes a leap!

With a wink and a nod, he waves goodnight,
Leaving all critters in laughter's delight.
Tomorrow's winks are bound to come,
For pranks in the woods are never done!

So if you hear giggles at the crack of dawn,
It's just old Woodrow playing a con.
Join the fun, let your worries wane,
Laughter in nature brings joy, not pain!

Lavender Laughter in Elven Quarters

In elven quarters where the lavender grows,
Fairies sprinkle giggles, as everyone knows.
One trip over petals, oh what a sight,
A bloom took a tumble, a goofy flight!

Elves sip their tea, while telling a joke,
A frog jumps by, and the teapot broke!
They laugh so hard, the daisies sway,
With laughter echoing, come what may.

They have a contest, who can laugh loudest,
While spiders weave webs, looking their proudest.
But with every giggle and wobbly stand,
There's joy enough to share, hand in hand.

So if you wander through that magical place,
Find the lavender laughter, join in the chase.
For in these quarters, joy's always near,
In every giggle, there's nothing to fear!

The Whims of Woodland Tricksters

The woodland tricksters are up to no good,
They's swapped the signs like only they could!
This tree says 'Gnome', that bush says 'Bear',
Now the sheep are frightened, in utter despair!

With jesters' hats and feathers galore,
They chase after rabbits, and dance on the floor.
Each tumble and slip sends them rolling away,
While the toadstools giggle at their silly display!

They paint the stones in colors so bright,
Causing old owls to hoot with delight.
But when the sun sets and the prank is revealed,
It's laugh-filled pandemonium, nothing concealed!

So, if you wander where the wild things play,
And hear a cackle or a giggle, stay!
For the woodland tricksters with their gleeful display,
Bring joy to the forest, come join the fray!

Veils of Laughter and Light

In a land where the giggles roam free,
A ticklish breeze hugs each silly tree.
Rabbits in hats, juggling with flair,
While cats serenade the delights in the air.

The sun wears a grin, oh so wide,
As shadows dance crazily with pride.
Pies fly by on a flight of dreams,
And laughter erupts like merry streams.

Rainbows roll out like vibrant rugs,
While snails tell jokes and give warm hugs.
Count the chuckles, it's simply the best,
In this whimsical world, we all are blessed.

So grab your hats, and let's all play,
For joy is the language of every day.
In veils of laughter, let's find the light,
Together we'll sparkle, oh what a sight!

Treasures of the Whispering Willow

Beneath the willow, secrets reside,
Where squirrels wear glasses and books are wide.
A treasure map scribbled on a leaf,
Leads to giggles instead of grief.

The fish in the pond swim with style,
Dressed in tuxedos, they dance for a while.
Raccoons play cards with mischief in mind,
While owls wrestle, their skills intertwined.

A treasure chest filled with candy and cheer,
Is guarded by gnomes who laugh with a sneer.
With each little giggle, the world gets bright,
In the whispers of willows, everything's light.

So let's roam together, friends side by side,
In the land where laughter and joy collide.
The willow knows secrets, it's time we gleam,
For treasures of laughter are our finest dream.

The Secret Recipe of Joy

A dash of giggles, a sprinkle of cheer,
Mix with the stardust flowing near.
Fold in some tickles, a touch of fun,
Bake at sunshine until it's done.

Add laughter whipped light, a swirl of delight,
Stir in some silly until it's just right.
A pinch of good vibes, a hug from a friend,
Taste it with smiles that never end.

Then pour out the platters, let's all take a bite,
Each morsel ignites a giggly delight.
With every flavor, the spirit will soar,
For joy is a recipe we can't ignore.

So share it with others, let laughter abound,
In this kitchen of life, let happiness sound.
The secret to joy, so simple, so clear,
Is finding the laughter that's always near.

The Gossamer Game

In fields of laughter, a game takes flight,
With whispers of fairies dancing at night.
Catch the giggles like butterflies rare,
While frogs hold court with royal flair.

The clouds are the players, so fluffy and bright,
Throwing oversized shadows that tickle with light.
Each jump creates ripples of joyful delight,
As the stars cheer on, twinkling so right.

Silly hats and shoes made of cheese,
Gather the friends, it's time to tease.
With each silly pose, the winners we crown,
In this gossamer game, we'll never frown.

So laugh out loud, and let spirits play,
For in this enchanted world, it's always the way.
With hearts wide open, and joy as our aim,
Let's dance together in this gossamer game!

The Art of Enchantment

In a garden of magic, gnomes come to play,
They sprinkle some laughter, chase clouds away.
With hats made of cabbage, they dance in the sun,
Claiming it's art, but we know it's just fun.

A wizard once dazzled with spells in a hat,
But tripped on his cloak and fell flat with a splat.
The toads all applauded, they laughed quite a lot,
For charm isn't magic, it's luck that you've got.

Fairies mix potions with quite a sly wink,
They brew them with giggles, then spill in the sink.
When asked for a favor, they usually grumble,
But a tickle will surely make any heart stumble.

So if you seek magic, take heed and be wise,
It's all in the laughter, not grand alibis.
When charms don't go right, just roll with the jest,
For the art of enchantment is humor at best.

Dance of the Twinkling Sprites

Beneath the full moon, the sprites come alive,
They twist and they turn, but can't seem to thrive.
With wings all a-twinkle, they giggle and spin,
Tripping on daisies, their dance wears them thin.

They swing from the branches, so graceful, so light,
But land on a snail, oh what a fright!
The snail, quite offended, begins to complain,
While the sprites just burble, 'We'll dance here again!'

One sprite lost her wig in the dance of the night,
It fluttered away; oh what a sight!
They chased it through meadows, they tumbled and rolled,

In the end, quite the spectacle — oh if truth be told!

So join in the frolic, let worries take flight,
For the dance of the sprites is a pure delight.
With laughter and charm, let's twirl in the mist,
'Cause who knows what magic a smile can assist?

Riddles in the Silver Mist

In the heart of the woods, where the silver mist lies,
A fox with a riddle caught all by surprise.
'What has keys but opens no locks?' said he,
A squirrel scratched his head, replied, 'Could it be me?'

The owl hooted softly, 'I've got one too,
What's sticky and sweet, yet not made of glue?'
A rabbit just chuckled and hopped up to say,
'If it's not a good joke, the punchline will stray!'

In riddles they babbled, the creatures all round,
Each twist and each turn was a tumbling sound.
'The answer's a giggle!' a badger then squealed,
And in fits of laughter, all worries were healed.

So if you encounter a riddle untried,
Just wrap it in humor, let joy be your guide.
For the riddles of life are to ponder and jest,
And laughter, dear friends, is what's truly the best!

Fables from the Fey Realm

In the fey realm where oddities reign,
A unicorn sneezed and let out a grain.
The fairies all giggled, they danced in a line,
For every good sneeze turns to laughter divine.

A troll with a temper was painting his wall,
But slipped on some paint and he started to fall.
With colors quite splattered and hair all askew,
He chuckled and said, 'Guess I'm modern art too!'

Once a pixie wished for a life made of cheese,
And woke up one morning with mice and with fleas.
So she fixed up her house with a sprinkle of flair,
And threw a grand party with crackers to share!

The fables from fey, they prickle and tease,
They remind us to laugh, and to do as you please.
For in every tall tale, there's a truth to behold,
A wink and a giggle, far better than gold.

Sprites and Shadows: The Prankster's Tale

In the forest where sprites play,
They sprinkle mischief every day.
With a giggle and a wink,
They'll make you spill your drink.

Shadowed paths where laughter springs,
They tug at shoes and steal your strings.
Watch your step, oh wandering fool,
For the sprite's quite the tricky tool.

They hide in bushes, snicker loud,
Creating chaos in the crowd.
One stole a hat, another a shoe,
And now they're dancing, just for you!

So next time when dusk settles in,
Beware the sprites' rascally grin.
For every chuckle, a prank's on the way,
In the forest where sprites love to play.

Laughter in the Enchanted Glade

In the glade where the fairies flit,
They spin their tales and little bits.
One tells a joke, another a pun,
Soon the whole glade is laughing and fun.

A gnome slips on a mushroom cap,
The fairies giggle, "What a trap!"
They scatter petals like confetti,
While the gnome just lands on his fretty.

With a twinkle, the moonlight plays,
Sprinkling laughter in a thousand ways.
Oh, the giggles and cheery glee,
In this enchanted glade, carelessly free.

So join the dance, don't be shy,
Laughter echoes beneath the sky.
In the heart of the glade, let joy reside,
With fairies and gnomes, side by side.

The Elusive Dance of Twilight Fae

In the twilight where fae do prance,
They weave through shadows in a dance.
One twirls here, another zips by,
They wink at you with a cheeky eye.

They trot on flowers, but oh so light,
Barely a whisper, quick as night.
If you blink, they're gone in a blink,
Leaving behind nothing but a wink.

With giggles echoing soft and genuine,
They tease the moon, their silver fountain.
You chase a shadow, they laugh and hide,
In the dance of dusk, they glide with pride.

So if you stumble upon their show,
Just laugh along, let your spirits flow.
For the fae of twilight are clever and sly,
Dancing in dreams as the night goes by.

Mischief Under the Starlit Canopy

Beneath the stars, the mischief brews,
Critters plotting with sneaky clues.
A raccoon with a bandit's mask,
And the owl's hoot is a clever task.

Up in the trees, the squirrels conspire,
Launching acorns with joyous fire.
Watch your head, oh wandering friend,
For acorn bombs are their latest trend!

The toads croak tunes with a silly beat,
While fireflies blink in a light-hearted feat.
Laughter bubbles up all around,
Under the canopy, joy is found.

So join the chaos, let your heart race,
Under the starlit canopy of grace.
For mischief awaits with a wink and a cheer,
In the magical night, let's spread the cheer!

Twilight Revelries: A Flora's Folly

In the garden at dusk, fairies take flight,
With dancing blooms that glow in the night.
A daisies' debate on who's the best dancer,
While the roses just pout, acting like prancer.

A sunflower shouts, "I'm the tallest of all!"
While the violets giggle, just having a ball.
They twirl and they leap, under bright moonbeams,
As the cat leaps and leaps, interrupting their dreams.

By the pond, there's a toad, with a top hat so tall,
Claiming he knows how to charm one and all.
With a croak and a wink, he calls them to play,
But they laugh at his tricks, then hop right away.

At twilight's sweet close, there are whispers of glee,
For in Flora's wild folly, all hearts would agree.
When laughter and blooms fill the shadowy vale,
The revelries thrive, in every detail.

The Trickster's Riddle by the Riverbank

Down by the river, a fox sits with glee,
Devise clever riddles, so witty, so free.
A fisherfolk mumbles, "Oh, not again!"
"What has teeth, but cannot bite, my friend?"

The fisherman scratches, his beard goes askew,
"Is it a... a comb?" The fox laughs anew.
With a twinkle in eye, he croons with delight,
"Riddle me this, do you think you'll get it right?"

An owl overhears, and hoots with disdain,
"Listen up, fishman! You're driving me insane!"
She swoops down with grace, as the trickster just smirks,
"What has six legs and always works?"

With finned friends in tow, they ponder and plot,
As the question spins round and round like a knot.
But laughter rings out as the river flows on,
For tricksters and riddles forever will dawn.

Glimpses of the Gallivanting Fae

In the woodland they flit, with their giggles and flair,
The gallivanting fae treat mischief with care.
They snatch all the acorns, then dress them in lace,
And swap them for marbles to join in the race.

A tiny blue sprite yells, "Who's fastest of all?"
With a wink and a whirl, they're off in a sprawl.
They scatter the dew, as they glide on a breeze,
Leaving behind giggles that dance with the trees.

One fairy named Tink, with a penchant for pranks,
Dresses a squirrel up in shiny clown ranks.
When the owl sees this, he cackles aloud,
As the creatures all gather, amazed by the crowd.

With flutters and flops, under stars they convene,
Sharing tales of the night and what might have been seen.

In glimpses of joy, through the moon's tender glow,
The fae dance and sing, with hearts all aglow.

Charmed Threads of an Elfin Tale

In a realm full of whimsy, where dreams intertwine,
Elves weave their stories, with laughter divine.
With needles made of starlight, and 'fetti for thread,
They stitch up their fables, as night softly spread.

One elf named Jingles, finds mischief so sweet,
Hiding socks in the flowers, oh what a treat!
He crafts tiny shoes, for the mice in a run,
While the daisies all giggle, thinking it's fun.

Beneath silver moonbeams, they gather in cheer,
With cups made of petals, and nectar to clear.
They toast to the tales and the magical nights,
As the lantern bugs dance, with their flickering lights.

So here's to the elves in their enchanted domain,
Whose threads weave a story, where joy's never plain.
Through charmed laughter and whimsy, their joy never fails,
For life is a tapestry of glittering tales.

Enchanted Eves and Bewitching Morns

The sun slips down with a sassy wink,
While munching cookies, I start to think.
The moon is laughing, painting the night,
Like a cheeky sprite in a costume fight.

Squirrels gossip about their grand schemes,
As owls join in with their wise old dreams.
Flowers bloom, bursting with scents galore,
All while my cat plots a garden tour.

Fairies sprinkle magic, it's quite absurd,
As my dog's convinced he's the wordy bird.
A breeze whispers secrets, oh such a tease,
I mumble back, hoping to impress the trees.

At dawn they giggle, start their charade,
With sunbeams flickering like a parade.
I sip my coffee, it spills on my lap,
And join the laughter—it's all a mishap!

The Chronicles of the Playful Pixies

In the garden where mischief doth bloom,
Pixies dance 'round with a brightly lit broom.
They giggle and twirl as they sprinkle cheer,
While my shoes trip over, oh dear, oh dear!

Their wings shimmer golden, a sight to behold,
Stealing my socks with a grin quite bold.
They toss them in air like confetti divine,
While I chase shadows, sipping on brine.

With every flitter and every small cheer,
Their laughter grows louder, it's too much, I fear!
They pluck away daisies and hide them with glee,
Leaving me barefoot and buzzing with "why me?"

At twilight they whisper their secrets to stars,
As I sit in the moonlight, counting my scars.
Who knew mischief could come in such forms?
Oh playful pixies, you'll usher my storms!

Mischief Under the Twinkling Stars

Beneath the night, the mischief begins,
With moonbeams and giggles, the laughter spins.
A cat in a hat joins in with delight,
While a raccoon plays drums in the pale moonlight.

The owls keep watch with their wise little heads,
As the hedgehog claims he can dance on his treads.
They twirl and they tumble, a whimsical mess,
While I sip my cocoa in utter distress.

Suddenly, a bat with a grumpy old frown,
Joins the dance to turn my world upside down.
A frog plays the lute, serenading the sky,
And I trip on my shoelace with an awkward sigh.

But laughter erupts from the stars far above,
As I join the frolic, forgetting to shove.
Under twinkling stars, where the night's full of fun,
We'll dance 'til the morning, till rising sun!

The Puckish Pursuit

In the garden of giggles, a chase does ensue,
Where a sprite with a grin has stolen my shoe.
I stumble and tumble, but oh what a sight,
As the sprite flicks her tail, darting out of sight.

With fairies a'flitting and mischief a'plenty,
I chase through the flowers, my dreams far from friendly.
They laugh as they hide all my cheese from the hunt,
Their chaotic delight is a mischievous stunt.

A gnome on a tricycle joins in for the fun,
As we whiz 'round the garden till faith is undone.
"Stop, little sprite!" I triumphantly call,
But she's off in a flash, laughing over it all.

Under the moonlight, the chase reaches peak,
I tumble and fumble, it's laughter I seek.
Yet who knew pursuit could be such a treat,
With sprites and gnomes making my evening complete!

Milton Keynes UK
Ingram Content Group UK Ltd.
UKHW010227111224
452348UK00011B/561